# Boxing

## Your Comprehensive Guide To Boxing Punches, Footwork, Head Movement & Combinations

## 1st Edition

By Frank Sasso

for any reparation, damages, or monetary loss due to the information herein, either directly or indirectly.

Respective authors own all copyrights not held by the publisher.

The information herein is offered for informational purposes solely, and is universal as so. The presentation of the information is without contract or any type of guarantee assurance.

# Table of Contents

# Introduction

Before we delve deep into the specifics of boxing, I want to thank you and congratulate you for purchasing this book.

Very few people end up taking action and pursuing their goals or dreams – by obtaining a copy of my book you've taken the first step in turning your desire to learn how to box into a reality.

You've spent a portion of your hard-earned cash and you've acquired what I deem to be the ultimate guide to boxing, regardless of how limited or competent you deem your current skillset to be.

Thanks again for purchasing this book, I truly hope you enjoy it!

But please remember, once you turn the last page of my book it's all on you to follow through and put the drills, exercises and techniques elaborated upon in this book to action... I can give you all the information, but YOU must put in the work...

You won't get better at any skill by not doing it.

# <u>First of all, what actually is boxing?</u>

A good old fashioned fist fight. Pro boxers are equipped with hand wraps and a pair of 8oz – 10oz lace up gloves while they attempt to score a knock out or technical knock out (referee stoppage) by throwing combinations of straight punches, hooks and uppercuts.

Boxing is often referred to as 'the sweet science', to the untrained eye boxing may appear as a primitive combat sport – with two guys trying to knock each other's head off their shoulders with little regard for anything else. To the boxing connoisseur it's a work of art. It wasn't until I embarked on my own boxing journey that I could truly develop an appreciation for the intricate details such as the precise head movement, the angles, the offensive and defensive footwork – the stance switches and circling.

Boxing isn't quite like Muay Thai – one well-placed right hand to the chin and it's likely lights out, as such boxers utilize a high guard, the Philly shell and a number of other elusive techniques to avoid taking any damage in the ring.

It's a game of making your opponent miss then immediately making them pay.

In Muay Thai, MMA and Karate it's rare to see a decorated athlete in the sport with zero losses on their record, in boxing the greats will preserve their undefeated record at all costs.

To this day boxing remains to provide boxers with the biggest pay days in combat sports – with millions of dollars being won and lost on the precise placement of straight punches and check hooks.

# Chapter 1 – How To Throw Straight Punches, Hooks & Uppercuts

Some of the drills we'll be performing in the later chapters of this book are purely footwork, while others involve footwork while throwing strikes (on focus mitts, at a partner and while shadowboxing). As such I thought we'd go through a bit of a refresher on our punches. At the end of the day great footwork isn't anywhere near as effective if you can't make your opponent pay with well executed strikes.

Let's take a look at the jab, straight right, left hook, right hook, left uppercut, right uppercut and shovel hook.

These punches form our bread and butter, keep in mind that there are multiple variations of each of these punches (i.e. the corkscrew jab, the body jab, a tight left hook, a looping overhand right) however for the purpose of this book we'll be covering the standard variation of each of these punches.

# The Jab

Start with your elbows tucked in (pointing down) and your gloves tucked up against your cheeks.

Extend your lead hand (left for orthodox stance, right for southpaw) as you drive through your hips.

Ensure your left hand doesn't drop at all during your punching motion – it should take the shortest path possible from in front of your face to the focus mitt/bag/opponent you are striking.

Before your arm reaches full extension rotate your fist until your knuckles are horizontal to your boxing rings canvas.

Once your jab lands bring your left glove straight back to your cheek.

If throwing a double jab instead of bringing your left glove straight back to your face opt to bring it about halfway back before rotating through the hips once again and throwing another jab.

## The Cross

Start with your elbows tucked in (pointing down) and your gloves tucked up against your cheeks.

Extend your rear hand (right for orthodox stance, left for southpaw) as you drive through your hips.

Ensure your right hand doesn't drop at all during your punching motion – it should take the shortest path possible from in front of your face to the focus mitt/bag/opponent you are striking (this is often referred to as throwing a punch 'down the pipe').

Before your arm reaches full extension rotate your fist until your knuckles are horizontal to your boxing rings canvas.

Once your cross lands bring your right glove straight back to your cheek.

# The Left Hook

Start with your elbows tucked in (pointing down) and your gloves tucked up against your cheeks.

Begin by twisting your hips slightly to the left to load up your power.

Ensuring your left glove doesn't drop at all while doing so proceed to throw your left hand in a short hooking motion directly to your adversaries' chin, ensuring your elbow remains slightly bent. Pivot your lead (left) foot inward while twisting your hips (which should be loaded to the left) back to the right.

There's a lot of debate as to which way your knuckles should be facing when the strike lands – from my experience it comes down to personal preference… landing your left hook with your knuckles facing either horizontal or parallel to the canvas in your boxing ring is a matter of what feels more natural to you.

Once your hook lands successfully immediately return your left glove to your cheek.

## The Right Hook

Start with your elbows tucked in (pointing down) and your gloves tucked up against your cheeks.

While pivoting on your rear right foot generate power through your hips by twisting them to the right.

Ensuring your right glove doesn't drop at all while doing so proceed to throw your right hand in a hooking motion directly to your adversaries' chin while your elbow remains slightly bent.

There's a lot of debate as to which way your knuckles should be facing when the strike lands – from my experience it comes down to personal preference... landing your right hook with your knuckles facing either horizontal or parallel to the canvas in your boxing ring is a matter of what feels more natural to you.

Once your hook lands successfully immediately return your right glove to your cheek.

The right hook is a extremely powerful and potentially fight ending punch if you're able to land it successfully, however the biggest issue is the right hook is quite easily telegraphed – your opponent can see a right hook coming from a mile away compared to your jab, straight right and left hook.

# The Shovel Hook

Start with your elbows tucked in (pointing down) and your gloves tucked up against your cheeks.

Take a small half step with your left foot while subtly 'loading' your hips tips to the left – this is where your devastating power is going to come from for this body shot.

Now begin to throw your left hand while pivoting back your lead foot and hips back to the right, aiming your glove for your opponent's floating rib.

There's a lot of debate as to which way your knuckles should be facing when the strike lands – from my experience it comes down to personal preference... landing your left hook with your knuckles facing either horizontal or parallel to the canvas in your boxing ring is a matter of what feels more natural to you.

Once your hook lands successfully immediately return your left glove to your cheek.

# The Left Uppercut

Start with your elbows tucked in (pointing down) and your gloves tucked up against your cheeks.

In one fluid motion lower your left shoulder slightly as your left glove drops down several inches (no need to lower it to your waist level) before driving through your hips and pivoting on your front (left) foot.

Fire your left glove from its slightly lowered position directly to underneath your opponents chin – generating as much power from the pivot as possible.

The second your punch lands return your left glove back to your cheek.

## The Right Uppercut

Start with your elbows tucked in (pointing down) and your gloves tucked up against your cheeks.

In one fluid motion lower your right shoulder slightly as your right glove drops down several inches (no need to lower it to your waist level) before driving through your hips and pivoting on your rear (right) foot.

Fire your right glove from its slightly lowered position directly to underneath your opponent's chin – generating as much power from the pivot as possible.

The second your punch lands return your right glove back to your cheek.

# Chapter 2 – The Importance of Footwork in Boxing

The vast majority of guys believe that boxing is all about the punching, ducking, weaving and slipping and first of all let me say I agree that footwork itself can't send your opponent crashing down against the ropes or leave them with a bad hematoma that prevents them from coming out for the next round... but it certainly sets you up to be in position to land that fight finishing combo.

Let's break down the big benefits of footwork when it comes to boxing, be it at the amateur level, professional level or even just moving around and hitting focus mitts with your friends.

## Your Footwork Is The Ultimate Defense

When the topic of defense in boxing is discussed the first few thing that often comes to mind are blocks, the parry and head movement... don't get me wrong yes these are the staples when it comes to protecting yourself in the ring but at the same time with well-developed footwork you won't be in a position that'll allow your adversary to strike from an angle that would require you to block or cover up.

In later chapters of this book, I'll elaborate on some of the boxing greats with the best footwork, watch some of their fights and you'll soon see it's almost as if their opponent is fighting a ghost – one moment they're in your face teeing off with hard, well timed shots... a split second later and they're gone.

Think about it, would you rather have to cover up and weather the storm or would you rather be out of the storm's way?

## Your Footwork will Allow You To Find & Exploit Angles

Great footwork creates great angles, and great angles place you in a position to land those round winning and fight finishing punches.

It's quite rare to land a knockout punch while standing directly in front of your opponent, unless you possess a sizeable speed advantage and happen to land a counter flush on your opponent's chin.

That's where angles come in. The subtle step off to the side, allowing you to blast that shovel hook to the body, the left foot pivot while you unload a check hook (pivoting lead hook) on an aggressive opponent who is attempting to back you up against the ropes.

## Your Footwork Will Help You Generate Power

True power comes when you learn to sit down on your punches, in order to sit down on your punches (sinking your weight into the canvas of the boxing ring) you must be well balanced in your stance. If you're leaning forward or have your weight distribution incorrect, you'll either miss and potentially fall forward (or sideways if it's a hook that is being thrown). Sitting down on your punches and always being in a position to counter with power will come as a result of performing the drills within this book.

Think about it, if your opponent throws a wild punch and misses, leaving their chin completely exposed for a moment and you have your legs crossed over or are standing too tall you will miss your opportunity to make them pay.

## Your Opponent Will Begin To Fatigue & Doubt Themselves

Trust me on this one, I've been on both sides of this statement. As a young up and comer sparring far more experienced men I would find myself with thoughts of dread, doubt and anger mid-round as I was repeatedly getting tagged by my sparring partner, every single time I tried to back them up against the corner of the ropes they'd disappear! My mind was fatigued trying to compute why I couldn't catch them and my legs were beginning to run out of gas as I hadn't put in the time performing footwork drills and roadwork like they had to build up the necessary endurance.

Now, after years of drills, road work, time in the ring and time spent studying the greats of boxing I'm the unhittable ghost. Sparring an individual that pays no attention to developing their footwork is like boxing in 3D while your opponent is only 2D. That's right, footwork adds a whole other dimension to the game.

Your opponent only sees straight lines – moving directly forward to attack and moving directly backwards to defend and retreat. You see much, much more.

## Your Footwork Will Allow You To Optimize Your Energy Expenditure

Firstly, it should come as no surprise, getting hit (particularly to the body) will sap the life out of you, efficient footwork means you'll take far less damage and thus be able to optimize your energy expenditure while increasing the volume of punches being thrown per round.

Secondly, when sparring a particularly aggressive opponent (the Mexican constant forward pressure style of fighting) it can be absolutely exhausting being on your back foot for multiple rounds – instead of moving backwards in a straight line opting to use your slick footwork to cut angles will allow you to save a large amount of your gas tank while frustrating your overly aggressive adversary.

## You'll Have Superior Leg Endurance From Performing Your Drills

It's all well and good that your punching and upper body endurance are on point, but in those deep dark later rounds of a bout if your leg endurance isn't up to scratch you'll find your defensive footwork becomes sloppy and you lack the energy to really sit down on your punches to do damage.

Although you may find a few of the drills repetitive and not overly fun to perform they'll be forging the leg endurance that may be the difference between you getting your hand raised and you leaving the ring with a loss on your record.

# Chapter 3 – Boxing Footwork Drills

On the following pages you'll find a wide variety of boxing footwork drills that're great for beginners, intermediate boxers, and even seasoned veterans.

Regardless of whether you've spent 10 minutes or 10 years in the ring these footwork drills if performed often will take your boxing to the next level.

## Boxing Footwork Drill #1 – Stance Switching Jump Rope

Begin with a jump rope, start with your left foot forward and your right foot back. With each rotation of your jump rope alternate between orthodox stance and southpaw stance (as you jump place your right foot forward and your left foot back).

Perform stance switches with your jump rope for rounds of 3 minutes.

## Boxing Footwork Drill #2 – Jab Cross Forwards & Back

This was the first boxing footwork drill I was taught many moons ago and it remains a staple, as a beginner this is an excellent drill to get your punches and footwork 'connected' so to speak.

If you're a complete beginner this drill can be a little frustrating to begin with as you know what steps etc. you want to take but when you go to perform it you mis-step or throw the wrong punch.

This all comes down to repetition, spend time on this drill and you shall be rewarded.

Begin by stepping forward with your lead leg (left for orthodox, right for southpaw) while throwing a jab.

Immediately step forward with your rear leg (right for orthodox, left for southpaw) while throwing a cross.

Now that you've taken two steps forward it's time to take two steps back while repeating the same…

Step back with your rear foot (right for orthodox, left for southpaw) while throwing a jab.

Immediately proceed to step back with your lead foot (left for orthodox, right for southpaw) while throwing your straight right hand.

You should now be in the same position you started in.

Repeat for rounds of 3 minutes.

# Boxing Footwork Drill #3 – The Cone 3 Punch Drill

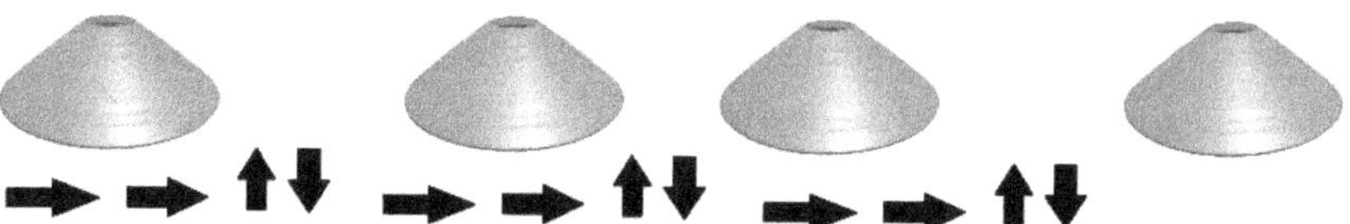

For this drill you'll need to set up 4 markers in a horizontal line with approximately 1 meter between each.

For this drill you'll be stepping in between each cone, throwing a 3 punch combo comprised of a jab, cross and left hook before taking two steps back, stepping laterally and repeating between the next cone or witches hat.

Once you've reached the end of your line of cones proceed to laterally step in the opposite direction, repeating your 3 punch combo until you're back to your starting position  - this counts as 1 round.

# Boxing Footwork Drill #4 – The Straight Punch Check Hook Drill

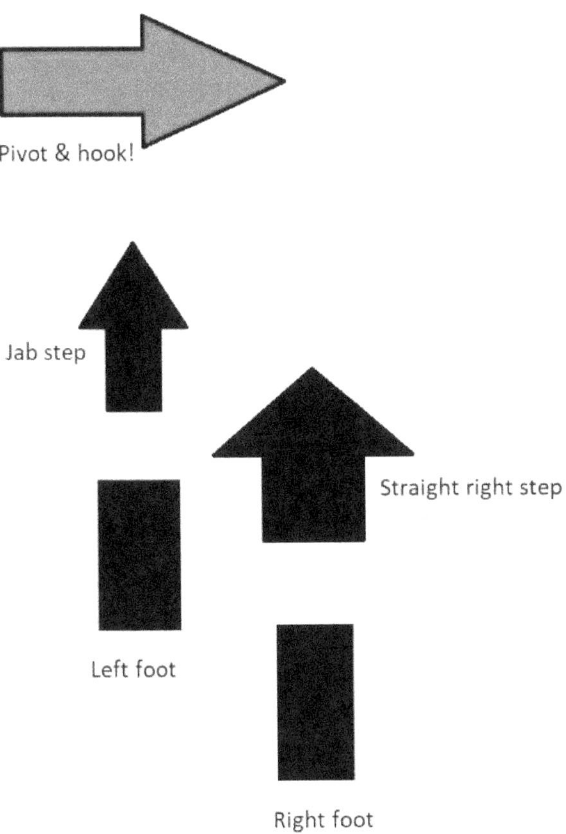



No equipment required for this drill! Simply ensure you have a few square meters of space to step and pivot.

Begin by taking a step forward with your lead foot while throwing a jab, followed by stepping your rear foot forward while throwing a straight right.

Now, here comes the fun part – the check hook. Imagine after throwing your jab cross combo that an aggressive opponent is stepping towards you – pivot on your front foot 90 degrees while throwing a short left hook.

Continue to throw your straight punches while continuing to pivot while throwing your lead hook.

**Boxing Footwork Drill #5 – Step 'N' Drag**

This is a basic yet effective drill to ensure you're never caught off balance or stepping incorrectly.

Begin in your regular boxing stands with your hands up by your cheeks.

Take a step in any direction with your front on your back foot.

Swiftly slide your other foot into position so you're back in your boxing stance.

Continue to take small steps with your lead and rear foot in various direction, immediately dragging your other foot to return to your boxing stance.

However far you move with one foot is the same distance you should move with the other to ensure you're always in your optimal boxing stance.

**Boxing Footwork Drill #6 – The Stance Switching Strike**

I recommend performing Drill #1 with your jump rope until you are happy with your stance switching movement.

You can either perform this drill in a shadowboxing fashion or have a training partner hold a pair of focus mitts for you.

Begin in your orthodox boxing stance and take three small steps forward while throwing a triple jab – no need to place a great deal of power behind your jab in this drill, your jab should be fast and act as a range finder.

After throwing your your third jab immediately switch to a southpaw stance by stepping your right foot forward and throw a straight right (which, now you've switched stances will also be your left hand).

Regardless of whether you're a an orthodox or southpaw boxer perform this drill from both stances, switching to the alternating stance.

Either perform a stance switch from regular to southpaw and then follow up your next combo going from southpaw to regular or opt to perform 3 minute rounds of each stance switch.

# Boxing Footwork Drill #7 – Plyometric Box Jumps

When it comes to building extreme power and speed in your legs the box jump is the go-to exercise. It's all well and good to repeat stance switching drills and the like but if your legs are lacking power and speed your adversary will take advantage of this in the ring.

I do not recommend using a metal framed plyometric box for your box jumps as I've seen far too many guys in the gym end up injured with sliced up shins thanks to these. Instead opt for a soft box that will be forgiving in case you fail to clear the box on your later repetitions as your legs begin to fatigue.

When it comes to plyometric box jumps you can perform them in various formats – for time, for a prescribed number of reps etc.

My personal favorite way to implement box jumps specifically for boxers to develop those fast explosive legs is the Tabata method.

Tabata training is a form of high-intensity interval training comprised of 20 seconds of work followed by 10 seconds of rest for a 4 minute period. Therefore, one round of Tabata is comprised of 8 rounds of 20 seconds of your box jumps.

Alternatively perform 30 seconds of box jumps followed by 30 seconds of rest until you reach a desired number of total repetitions (i.e. 100, 200).

# Boxing Footwork Drill #8 – Agility Ladder In 'N' Outs

For the In 'N' Out drill you will require an agility ladder, if you don't own or have access to an agility ladder simply use some tape or chalk and draw a bunch of boxes on the floor to replicate the look of an agility ladder.

Begin with both feet inside the first square of your agility ladder before stepping outside of the ladder with your left foot, then your right foot before placing your left foot then your right foot inside the second square of your agility ladder. Proceed stepping inside and outside the squares of your agility ladder with your feet until you reach the end of the ladder, then it's time to do it in reverse (going backwards!).

# Boxing Footwork Drill #9 – Agility Ladder Forward & Back

For the forward & back drill you will require an agility ladder, if you don't own or have access to an agility ladder simply use some tape or chalk and draw a bunch of boxes on the floor to replicate the look of an agility ladder.

Chances are if you've watched or participated in agility ladder drills before you've seen or performed the forward & back drill, this is a personal favorite of mine and for good reason – it's excellent for building fluidity and dexterity of movement.

Begin by standing in front of your agility ladder.

As we'll begin by moving laterally to the left side of our ladder start by placing your left foot inside the square of your ladder, as you bring your right foot into the ladder bring your left foot outside of the ladder square.

On your next step you'll be stepping first with your right foot into the second square of your agility ladder, as you step into the second square of your agility ladder with your left foot bring your right foot outside of the agility ladder.

Repeat alternating left and right lateral movement until you reach the end of your ladder, then turn around and move your way laterally through the ladder again until you have returned to your starting position.

# Boxing Footwork Drill #10 – The Straight Punch Body Hook Pivot

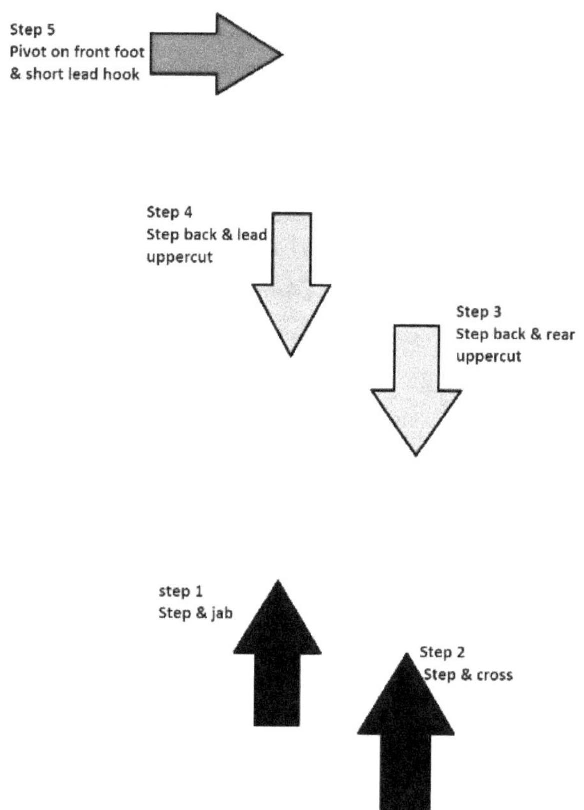



This boxing drill is comprised of a 5 punch combo that I regularly catch my opponents with in sparring, I highly recommend mastering this drill as if you're able to effortlessly punch going forwards, backwards and on a pivot you'll be trouble for any opponent in the ring... those that don't develop their footwork like you are have a pretty difficult time fighting off their back foot.

This drill can either be performed shadow boxing or on a pair of focus mitts with a training partner.

Begin in your orthodox boxing stance and take a small step forward with your left (lead) foot while throwing a jab. Immediately follow up with a small step forward with your right (rear) leg while throwing a right cross. Now we're going to pretend our adversary is on the offensive so we're going to take a step backward with our rear (right) foot while throwing a rear uppercut, then immediately taking a step back with your front foot while following up with a front uppercut.

End the combo by pivoting off to your left side 90 degrees while throwing a short left hook.

## Boxing Footwork Drill #11 – The Backwards Jump Rope

Jumping rope in the regular forward motion of the rope is easy as you can see exactly when you need to jump to clear the rope, you've got a simple visual cue… the same cannot be said for when it comes to rotating your jump rope backwards.

You have to go off of timing and feeling – both traits that must be mastered to take your boxing footwork to the next level.

I recommend performing longer rounds of 5 and 10 minutes while performing the backwards jump rope drill at a steady pace while also occasionally performing Tabata rounds of the backwards jump rope (20 seconds work, 10 seconds rest for 4 minutes).

## Boxing Footwork Drill #12 – Landing The Shovel Hook

Getting hit in the face is never fun but let me assure you getting hit with a perfectly placed body shot is honestly that much worse! Speaking of body shots this drill is going to focus on landing a perfectly placed shovel hook on your opponent's rib cage.

Here's the thing – unlike our straight punches and regular left hook it's near impossible to land the shovel hook while standing directly in front of your opponent… we need to cut the right angle to blast that powerful hook to their midsection.

Here's how to do it…

Begin by throwing a jab, feinting a jab, throwing another jab and then while feinting a jab for the second time take a step to the left with your lead foot while loading your hips to the left.

From here we'll drive that lead hand shovel hook directly to where your imaginary adversaries rib cage would be.

Take a step back with your lead leg to return to your boxing stance before moving around and repeating this drill.

## Boxing Footwork Drill #13 – The X

For this drill you'll require 5 cones or 5 pieces of tape placed on the floor to form a X. Essentially make a square with 4 cones and place one cone in the middle.

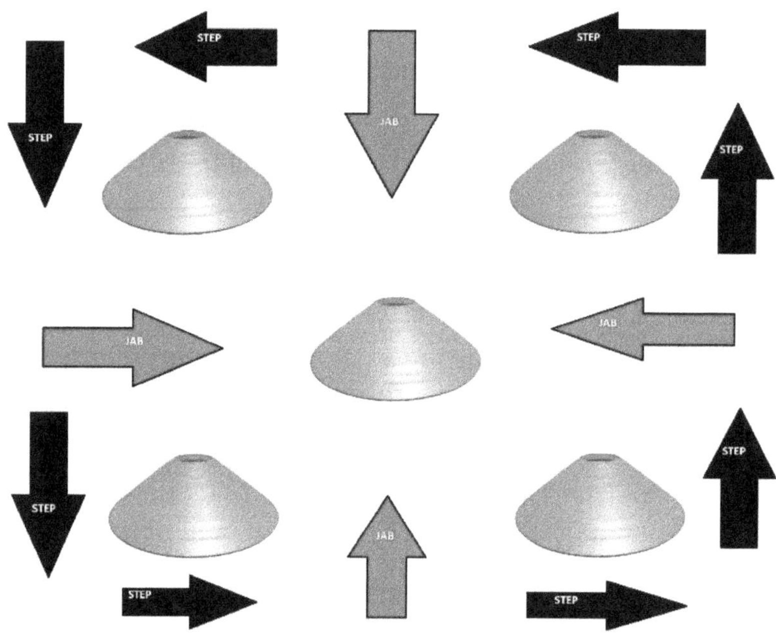


Begin by circling around your cones by stepping laterally, step in between the gap of the cones (your front foot should almost be touching the cone placed in the middle) and throw a jab before stepping back out and circling to the next opening in your cones and repeating this same jab, step out and lateral movement pattern.

When performing multiple rounds of this drill alternate the direction you are circling around the cones each round (i.e. round 1 should be clockwise, round 2 should be counter clockwise).

# Boxing Footwork Drill #14 – The Cone Circle

For this drill you'll require 9 cones, witches hats or 9 pieces of tape placed on the floor. Create a circle using 8 comes while placing the 9ᵗʰ cone in the middle of your circle.

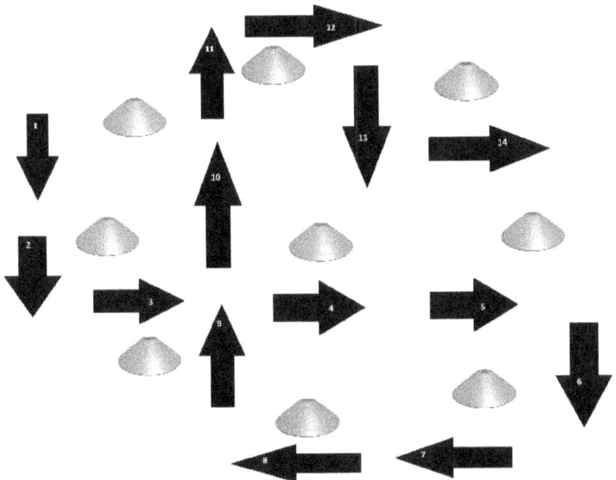

Unlike the previous 'X' drill utilizing cone which involves methodically working your way into the gap between each cone when it comes to our cone circle drill it's extremely dynamic.

That's right, we aren't going to be going in and out of each and every cone – instead opt to move laterally around the outside of some of the cones before stepping in the middle and throwing a two or three punch boxing combination of your choice before moving out the opposite side on an angle. Proceed to move around the outside of your cones again, step in and throw a combo before exiting between another set of cones on an angle and so forth.

# Boxing Footwork Drill #15 – The 90 Degree Uppercut Drill

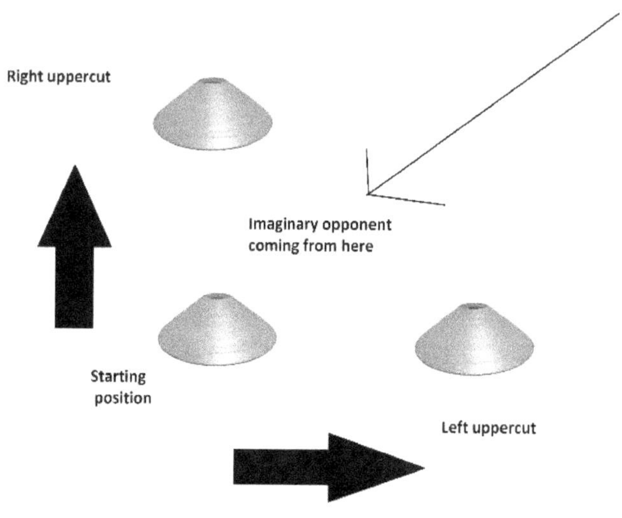


For this drill you'll require 3 cones, witches hats or 3 pieces of tape placed on the floor to create a 90 degree angle (essentially the shape of the letter L).

This drill is designed to cut an angle and land an uppercut on an opponent coming towards you with straight punches – we're going to be performing this drill using both orthodox and southpaw stances.

Hop laterally from your left side of your cones to the right side of your and throw a left uppercut (the hand closest to the middle cone). Immediately hop laterally from the right side of your cones to the left side of your cones and throw a right uppercut (the hand closest to the middle cone).

Continue to repeat this drill for the desired number of repetitions, imagining your opponent is coming at you through the path of your middle cone and you're continuing to cut angles from both the orthodox and southpaw stance as you rip away with your inside uppercuts.

# Boxing Footwork Drill #16 – The Tape Square Drill

For this drill you guessed it! You'll need some tape.
Begin by taping 9 squares on the floor (all joined together)
each square should be approximately the size of your foot.

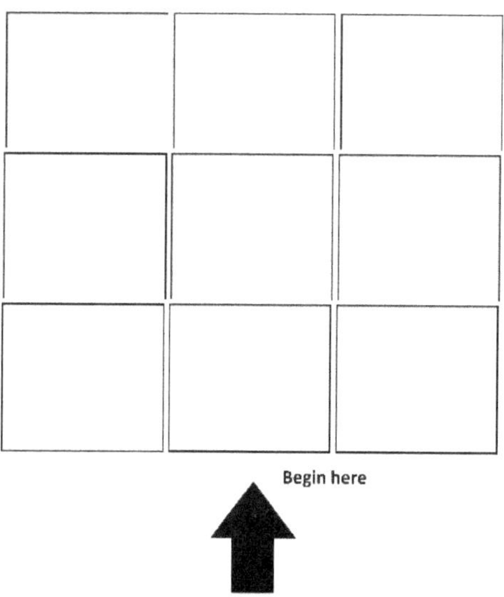



Begin standing behind the middle of the 3 squares at the back
– step forward and throw a jab – your front should now be
inside one of the squares. Continue to move forward, laterally
to both the left and right as well as moving backwards as you
step between your 9 tape squares, throwing a punch with your
left hand when you step left (this could be a lead hook, left
uppercut or jab) and throwing a punch with your right hand
when stepping right (this could be a right hook, straight right
or rear uppercut).

This is a fantastic drill to understand how far you should be
stepping on each punch not to mention an excellent way to
ensure you're always in your correct boxing stance after
throwing a punch.

**Boxing Footwork Drill #17 – The Jab Cross Puppet Drill**

No equipment (or space) required whatsoever for this drill, we're going to perform this one on the spot.

The best cue to understand this drill and to ensure you're performing it correctly is to imagine that you are a string puppet. Your left hand is connected to your left foot via a string and your right hand is connected to your right foot via a string.

Begin by throwing a jab while lifting your left foot up, your left foot should return to the floor as your jab reaches its full extension. Proceed to throw a straight right hand while picking up your right foot, once again return your right foot to the floor as your straight right hand reaches its full extension.

Alternate throwing your jab and cross while lifting your left and right foot in sync with your punches.

Perform for rounds of 3 minutes.

## Boxing Footwork Drill #18 – The 3 Punch Pivot

The only requirement for this boxing footwork drill is tape or
some chalk to draw 4 equal sized boxes on the floor.

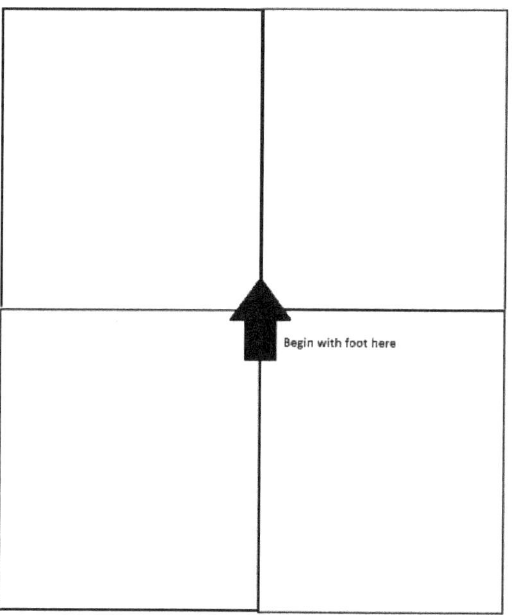


Begin in your boxing stance with your lead foot positioned on
the middle line where all 4 boxes intersect. From here you'll
begin by pivoting to the left on the ball of your lead foot.

Immediately throw a 3 punch combination, some examples of
combos you may like to use include:

Jab – cross – left hook

Jab – jab – right uppercut

Left uppercut – right uppercut – left hook

Right uppercut – left hook – straight right

As soon as you've thrown your combo proceed to pivot again 90 degrees on your lead leg, ensuring your foot is on the middle line of the 4 boxes before throwing your next 3 punch combo.
Continue to pivot and throw a variety of 3 punch combos for rounds of 3 minutes each.

# Boxing Footwork Drill #19 – Hoppers

The only way to improve your endurance and current ability is to push yourself beyond your current limitations… that's what we're going to be doing with these hoppers, your quads, hamstrings, calves… your lower body is going to feel like it's on fire after a solid 3 to 5 minute set of hoppers! Push through the temporary pain and reap the rewards on the other side.

No equipment required for this footwork drill (with the exception of some mental fortitude).

Begin by dropping down low as if you were performing a bodyweight squat.
Place your hands on your head and position yourself on the balls of your feet while you maintain your squat position.

Begin to perform small bounces on your toes, you can opt to remain in one spot or move around while bouncing on your toes (while remaining in your low squat position). This is one of the ultimate drills for building up that leg endurance.

**Boxing Footwork Drill #20 – Shadowboxing Down Low**

Once you've mastered the tough yet rewarding hoppers drill mentioned on the previous page it's time to add onto the hopping motion and add in some shadowboxing! That's right – remove your hands from your head and perform combos of between 2 and 4 punches while bouncing on your toes, opting to occasionally pivot and change directions as well as moving forward and back.

Notice how much harder it is to shadowbox down low than if you were standing?
That's the exact purpose of this drill – to put you through the hard yards in training so when you stand up and compete against an adversary your endurance, balance and movement as a whole are that much better.

Perform your shadowboxing for multiple rounds of 3 minutes while ensuring you remain bouncing on your toes in your low squat position for the duration of each round.

## Boxing Footwork Drill #21 – The Ali Shuffle

Considering you're reading a book on boxing the Ali shuffle should require no introduction.
Begin with your hands held up high against your chin and begin alternating between fast and slow bursts of sliding your left foot back and your right foot forward and vice versa.

Far more than just a display of show boating, the Ali Shuffle can confuse your opponent in the ring and is a great drill to increase the speed and fluidity of your footwork.

I personally like to use the Ali shuffle in a Tabata style workout – performing 20 seconds of fast Ali shuffles before immediately performing 10 seconds of slow Ali shuffles – repeating for 4 minutes.

**Boxing Footwork Drill #22 – The Slip Rope Drill**

For this slip rope drill you'll need to hang a piece of string or rope that is approximately 4 metres in length at neck height, as if we set our slip rope too heigh you'll often become lazy with your head movement.

This drill is as old as the hills but is great for working on evasive footwork and head movement.

Begin on the right side of your slip rope, take a small step forward with your lead foot while throwing a jab followed by a small step forward with your rear leg while throwing a straight right.

Slip under your string or rope and take another two small steps while you throw your jab and straight right.

Proceed to slip under alternating sides of your rope while throwing your straight punches.

Once you make it to the end of the rope either opt to turn around and repeat the drill or if you're feeling up to it perform your steps, slips and straight punches while going backwards.

# Chapter 4 – The Importance of Head Movement in Boxing

The vast majority of guys believe that boxing is all walking forward and winging punches at your opponent, if they end up backed up against the ropes in a compromising position perhaps they'll cover up with a tight guard and absorb a few punches until they're able to find their way off the ropes.

Developing your boxing head movement will improve your defense, offense and longevity in the ring – let's delve in a bit deeper and look at the benefits you can reap by developing your head movement, be it at the amateur level, professional level or even just moving around and hitting focus mitts with your friends.

## Head Movement Allows You To Immediately Go On The Offensive

Think about it, when you're covering up to block your opponents strikes, be it with a high guard, a block or a parry your gloves are focused entirely on mitigating damage from your opponents strikes – they're not in position at all to go on the offensive.

When you utilize head movement in your defense you'll find that your hands can be in position to strike, this embodies the old 'Make them miss and make them pay' ideology.

Here's an example – imagine your opponent has you backed up in the ring, you anticipate that a lead uppercut is about to come your way, as such you shell up – your opponents uppercut doesn't land flush but it still does a little bit of damage... however your hands are in no position to retaliate or fire back and as a result of this you eat a barrage of punches and throw zero in return.

Blocking and covering up is for survival and for those who have not worked on developing proficient head movement.

Now, let's run through the same scenario with head movement as our primary defensive maneuver as opposed to blocking or covering up.

Once again, your opponent has you backed up in the ring, you suspect a lead uppercut is about to head straight to your chin so you slip your head to the outside – off the center line as your opponent throws their strike.

As your head isn't there to be hit your opponent over extends and finds themselves in a compromised position, as your hands weren't occupied you're able to immediately throw a powerful left hook, ending the bout.

## Head Movement Helps Form A Path To Victory Against More Athletic Opponents

Stay in the sport long enough and regardless of how athletic you deem yourself to be you'll always come across an opponent that has a speed advantage on you, it's inevitable. Unless you're the faster guy, trading straight punches is not going to be a path to victory – you're going to have to negate their speed advantage with constant head movement and counters.

Foresee a wide right hook coming your way? Use your head movement to roll and immediately unload a straight right followed by a left hook of your own. As The Notorious Conor McGregor said "timing beats speed" – through the use of good head movement we can capitalize on these opportunities against faster opponents.

## Good Head Movement Can Mentally Break Your Adversary

I speak from my own experience, particularly as you begin to fatigue in the later rounds of your scheduled bout – when you put some power behind a punch and it fails to even graze your opponent the frustration is real… when that happens time and time again over the course of 1, 2 or 3 rounds it can mentally break you. You convince yourself that you simply can't hit your opponent and as such this prophecy remains true.

## Head Movement Can Get Your Opponent Reacting, Thus Creating Openings

The most common feint used to try and draw an attack or reaction out of your opponent is the jab, however this is only effective until it isn't – after a round or two your opponent will have likely picked up on your feinting action and no longer react to it – that's when we can begin implementing our head movement to try and draw an attack out of our opponent will having our counter loaded and ready to go.

## Head Movement Increases Your Longevity

Regardless of whether you're participating in a one-off charity boxing match or lacing up your gloves to fight for your third world title you do not want to take any unnecessary punches – the length and success realized of Floyd Mayweather's boxing career is largely due to the fact he took almost no damage. If he went out there and fought like a rock 'em sock 'em robot there is no way he would've fought at the highest level for as long as he did.

# Chapter 5 – Boxing Head Movement Drills

On the following pages you'll find a wide variety of boxing head movement drills that're great for beginners, intermediate boxers, and even seasoned veterans.

Regardless of whether you've spent 10 minutes or 10 years in the ring these head movement drills, if performed often will take your boxing to the next level.

**Boxing Head Movement Drill #1 – The Mirror Drill**

Begin standing in front of a mirror in your boxing stance, have a friend or training partner draw the outline of your head on the mirror using an erasable marker.

You will be shadow boxing for rounds of 3 minutes each, your aim is to continuously throw combinations and perform defensive head movement maneuvers – your head should never marry up with the outline drawn on the mirror for more than 1 second at a time – this is a great drill to learn to keep your head off the center line.

## Boxing Head Movement Drill #2 – The Rope Bob 'N' Weave

Begin by attaching a rope or piece of string at chin height between 2 objects – aim for your extended string or rope to be anywhere between 5 and 10 meters in length.

You will start on the left side of your string or rope in your boxing stance and begin by throwing a jab followed by a cross before immediately weaving until to the right side of your string or rope.

You will continue to throw your straight punches while bobbing and weaving from left to right until you reach the end of your string or rope.

Turn around and work your way back to the starting position, this is 1 round.

I highly recommend performing this drill in both orthodox and south paw stances, although you may not utilize the opposite stance for your offense it's extremely beneficial to be defensively proficient from your opposite stance.

Should you wish to take this suggestion I recommend:

- Perform one round orthodox and immediately follow it up with one round southpaw.

- Perform the length of your string or rope orthodox and when turning around to return to your starting position perform the return trip in your opposite stance.

## Boxing Head Movement Drill #3 – Prepping The Power Shot

Begin by standing in your boxing stance in front of your heavy bag.
Begin peppering your heavy bag with constant jabs and crosses – no need to place any power behind these strikes, remain standing on the spot while you throw these punches – feel free to rotate through your hips but do not move.

After every 10th strike slip to the outside (left for orthodox) and throw a powerful lead uppercut.

Return your head to the center line and proceed to pepper your heavy bag with another 10 straight punches.

Alternate between throwing a lead uppercut, lead hook and shovel hook as you take your head off the center line and throw your powerful shot after 10 straight punches.

Repeat for rounds of 3 minutes each.

## Boxing Head Movement Drill #4 – Slow Sparring

For this drill you'll need a partner and each of you will require a pair of gloves and a mouthpiece.

When most guys think of sparring they think of what is essentially a fight, that's the complete opposite of what we're going for with this drill.

The objective here is to have your partner intentionally throw combinations of slow punches towards you, ensuring you see them so you're able to make an accurate read of where to move your head.

In a scheduled bout your adversary is most certainly not going to be slowing punches slowly, allowing you to move your head but by practicing this way you'll build familiarity with how to move your head when you anticipate a particular combo (i.e. jab, cross, hook, cross) coming your way.

**Boxing Head Movement Drill #5 – Ball Evasion**

For this drill we'll need some duct tape, a piece of rope and a tennis ball (if you don't have a tennis ball then a baseball or similar will do the trick).

Begin by duct taping the tennis ball to one end of your rope before taping the other end of your rope to your ceiling, the tennis ball should be at approximately chin level when hanging directly down from your ceiling.

From here we will be performing rounds of 3 minutes of evading our tennis ball while shadowboxing underneath it. Begin by swinging your tennis ball as if were a pendulum – throw straight punches, hooks and uppercuts while slipping, evading, and weaving under your tennis ball each time it swings by you.

Ensure you're also pivoting, changing directions etc. to make the ball evasion drill as dynamic as possible.

## Boxing Head Movement Drill #6 – Jab Evasion

The only requirement for the jab evasion head movement drill is a partner – no gloves or mouthguards necessary for this one (although feel free to use them if you wish!).

Your partner will be throwing jabs at you for rounds of 3 minutes each, we will be utilizing 4 different head movement techniques to evade the jab.

Upon your training partner throwing the first jab opt to slip to the left (the outside).

Upon your training partner throwing the second jab opt to slip to the right (the inside).

Upon your training partner throwing the third jab opt to lower your level in order to duck under the punch.

Upon your training partner throwing the fourth jab opt to use a pull, simply pulling your head back.

Continue to perform the following four evasive head movement techniques in order while your training partner continues to throw jabs for rounds of 3 minutes each.

**Boxing Head Movement Drill #7 – Moving In And Out Of Range**

For this drill you'll need a partner to be wearing a pair of boxing gloves.
The purpose of this drill is to work on using your evasive head movement to get in close range (often referred to as 'the pocket') of your opponent.

Have your partner begin with both of their arms directly extended in front of them.

Begin standing in your boxing stance to the left side of their extended left boxing glove. Begin by stepping to the right as you weave under their left glove – you should now be between their two extended arms. Once again, take a step to the right as you weave under their extended right arm. Now we'll be stepping to the left as we weave back under their right arm – perform rounds of 3 minutes as you continue to weave between your opponents extended arms.

Once you're comfortable performing this drill standing on the spot begin to have your partner alternate walking forwards for one round as you move backwards while weaving between their extended arms to get in range.

After performing one round of you moving backwards while your training partner moves forwards switch it up, have your training partner walk backwards with their arms extended while you move forwards while weaving into range.

**Boxing Head Movement Drill #8 – Head Movement Oriented Focus Mitt Drills**

For this drill you'll require a trainer partner wearing a pair of focus mitts.
Perform rounds of 3 minutes comprised of the following drills:

Focus Mitt Drill #1

Jab
Cross
Pad holder throws a hook, roll under it
Cross

Focus Mitt Drill #2

Pad holder throws a jab and cross, slip left and then right.
Jab
Cross
Pad holder throws a jab and cross, slip left and then right.
Cross

Focus Mitt Drill #3

Pad holder throws a cross, duck under it.
Right uppercut
Left uppercut
Pad holder throws a hook, roll under it
Left hook

Focus Mitt Drill #4

Jab
Cross
Hook
Pad holder throws a cross, slip it.
Pad holder throws a hook, roll under it.

**Boxing Head Movement Drill #9 – Pool Noodle Evasion**

This is a personal favorite of mine; I've been utilizing this exact drill in my boxing gyms for years and the sheer improvement I've seen in terms of head movement in the ring as a result of continuous drilling is immense.

For this drill you'll need a partner and a pair of foam pool noodles.

For rounds of 3 minutes in duration have your partner use the pool noodles to throw straight shots and hooks at you at a reasonable speed – you must attempt to slip, roll and duck under as many of these shots as possible. The beauty of using the pool noodles is we're able to throw the strikes faster and with more force behind them while at the same time if you fail to avoid a strike you won't get injured as the noodles are extremely forgiving.

**Boxing Head Movement Drill #10 – The Tennis Ball Drill**

This is an old school boxing head movement drill that although I haven't seen performed for a while it most certainly still works as a means of developing your boxing head movement, unfortunately I can't say it's quite as forgiving as the foam pool noodle drill.

For this drill you will need a training partner and a bucket of tennis balls, some guys also like to wear head gear when performing this drill.

Your training partner is to throw the tennis balls towards you at your head level, you will use head movement to evade one ball, then you will strike the second ball with a punch of your choice (e.g. jab, cross, left hook). Repeat striking and evading balls for rounds of 3 minutes or until your bucket is empty.

I recommend your training partner stands roughly 5 meters away from you when throwing the tennis balls.

## Boxing Head Movement Drill #11 – The Mike Tyson Bag Drill

For this drill you'll need a heavy bag, as we discussed earlier in the book Mike Tyson had absurdly good head movement – using the peek a boo style to get within range of his opponents and land damaging blows in the pocket.

For this drill we're going to be throwing a simple jab, cross, lead hook combo at our heavy bag however we're going to ensure we're using the peek a boo style head movement between each punch.

Begin by throwing a jab and moving your head to the right.
Now throw your cross and move your head to the left.
Throw a left hook as you move your head to the right.

Start of slow, taking a moment to throw each punch and ensure your head movement is correct with each punch before speeding it up, emulating Tyson's peek a boo style of constant movement while you begin to unload your 3 punch combo on the heavy bag.

Perform for rounds of 3 minutes on your heavy bag.

# Chapter 6 – Your Boxing Footwork Workouts

Now that I've shared with you 22 highly effective boxing footwork drills that I regularly perform and prescribe to my clients it's time to put them all together into a series of boxing footwork workouts.

Before I share my workouts with you let me start by saying these are just my examples, there's really no right or wrong way to structure your boxing footwork workout... grab a bunch of drills from this book and place them together into a workout by setting repetitions/rounds for each exercise to suit your liking.

Alternatively follow some of my examples below (sometimes I like to incorporate elements of explosive drills, endurance drills and technical drills all into one boxing foot workout, other times I might perform 3 boxing footwork workouts per week – with each workout focusing on one of these different areas.

**Boxing Footwork Workout #1 – Technical Focus**

Drill #3 – The Cone 3 Punch Drill – 3 rounds of 3 minutes per round

Drill #6 – The Stance Switching Strike - 3 rounds of 3 minutes per round

Drill #10 – The Straight Punch Body Hook Pivot - 3 rounds of 3 minutes per round

Drill #18 – The 3 Punch Pivot - 3 rounds of 3 minutes per round

**Boxing Footwork Workout #2 – Endurance Focus**

Drill #1 – Stance Switching Jump Rope – 3 rounds of 3 minutes per round

Drill #17 – The Jab Cross Puppet Drill – 3 rounds of 3 minutes per round

Drill #19 – Hoppers – 3 rounds of 3 minutes per round

Drill #20 – Shadowboxing Down Low – 3 rounds of 3 minutes per round

**Boxing Footwork Workout #3 – Explosive Power Focus**

Drill #7 – Plyometric Box Jumps – 5 rounds of 10 box jumps per round

Drill #21 – The Ali Shuffle – 3 rounds of 3 minutes per round

Drill #15 – The 90 Degree Uppercut Drill - 3 rounds of 3 minutes per round

Drill #8 – Agility Ladder In 'N' Outs - 3 rounds of 3 minutes per round

Drill #9 – Agility Ladder Forward & Back - 3 rounds of 3 minutes per round

## Boxing Footwork Workout #4 – Well Rounded

Drill #10 – The Straight Punch Body Hook Pivot - 3 rounds of 3 minutes per round

Drill #5 – Step 'N' Drag - 3 rounds of 3 minutes per round

Drill #3 – The Cone 3 Punch Drill - 3 rounds of 3 minutes per round

Drill #7 – Plyometric Box Jumps – 5 rounds of 10 box jumps

Drill #8 – Agility Ladder In 'N' Outs - 3 rounds of 3 minutes per round

## Boxing Footwork Workout #5 – Well Rounded

Drill #2 – Jab Cross Forwards & Back - 3 rounds of 3 minutes per round

Drill #11 – The Backwards Jump Rope - 3 rounds of 3 minutes per round

Drill #13 – The X – 3 rounds of 3 minutes per round

Drill #22 – The Slip Rope Drill – 3 rounds of 3 minutes per round

# Chapter 7 – Your Boxing Head Movement Workouts

**Boxing Head Movement Workout #1**
Drill #5 – Ball Evasion – 3 rounds of 3 minutes each
Drill #1 – The Mirror Drill – 3 rounds of 3 minutes each
Drill #11 – The Mike Tyson Bag Drill – 3 rounds of 3 minutes each
Drill #10 – The Tennis Ball Drill – 1 bucket of tennis balls

**Boxing Head Movement Workout #2**
Drill #9 – Pool Noodle Evasion – 2 rounds of 5 minutes each
Drill #7 – Moving In And Out Of Range – 3 rounds of 3 minutes each
Drill #8 – Head Movement Oriented Focus Mitt Drills – 5 rounds of 5 minutes each
Drill #4 – Slow Sparring – 3 rounds of 2 minutes each

**Boxing Head Movement Workout #3**
Drill #1 – The Mirror Drill – 3 rounds of 2 minutes each
Drill #2 – The Rope Bob 'N' Weave – 3 rounds of 2 minutes each
Drill #6 – Jab Evasion – 3 rounds of 2 minutes each
Drill #4 – Slow Sparring – 12 rounds of 1 minute each

**Boxing Head Movement Workout #4**
Drill #1 – The Mirror Drill – 3 rounds of 2 minutes each
Drill #2 – The Rope Bob 'N' Weave – 3 rounds of 2 minutes each
Drill #3 – Prepping The Power Shot – 3 rounds of 2 minutes each
Drill #4 – Slow Sparring – 3 rounds of 2 minutes each

**Boxing Head Movement Workout #5**
Drill #7 – Moving In And Out Of Range – 5 rounds of 2
minutes each
Drill #8 – Head Movement Oriented Focus Mitt Drills – 3
rounds of 5 minutes each
Drill #9 – Pool Noodle Evasion - 3 rounds of 2 minutes each
Drill #10 – The Tennis Ball Drill – 1 bucket of tennis balls

**Boxing Head Movement Workout #6**
Drill #2 – The Rope Bob 'N' Weave – 3 rounds of 2 minutes
each
Drill #9 – Pool Noodle Evasion - 3 rounds of 2 minutes each
Drill #11 – The Mike Tyson Bag Drill – 3 rounds of 3 minutes
each
Drill #3 – Prepping The Power Shot – 3 rounds of 2 minutes
each

# Chapter 8 – General Boxing Footwork Tips

Now that you are well informed on the benefits of developing your boxing footwork, you know the advantages to wearing boxing boots, you've had a refresher on how to throw your punches correctly not to mention you've been armed with a hefty number of boxing footwork drills lets run through some general boxing footwork tips and tricks that haven't fit into any of the previous chapters.

## Boxing Footwork Tip #1

Keep your body loose and relaxed.

I've coached guys with unbelievable cardio endurance when it comes to running, swimming, cycling and jumping rope... but as soon as they get in the boxing ring and start to move around with a partner they get fatigued extremely quickly.

Is this due to their cardio fitness not translating over to boxing? Not at all.
It's because they're remaining extremely stiff and tense while moving around the ring.

Remaining stiff and tense is a sure-fire way to empty your gas tank in a short period of time.

## Boxing Footwork Tip #2

Don't utilize too wide of a boxing stance.

It comes down to personal preference, but I personally recommend keeping your boxing stance fairly narrow – a narrow stance not only results in quicker lateral movement and pivots but it requires less energy too.

Trying to quickly change direction to get yourself off of the ropes or to pivot away from your opponent is slow, clunky and requires more energy. A lot of disadvantages and no real benefit (the only time I recommend a super wide and low stance is in the world of MMA when you have the classic striker vs. grappler match up).

## Boxing Footwork Tip #3

Maintain a straight spine.

A straight spine makes maintaining your balance while striking and evading your opponent that much easier – when leaning back or hunching forward and maintaining a stance heavy on your front leg it's that much harder to remain balanced – this results in excess energy expenditure and potentially weaker punches… remember if you're off balance there's no way to sit down on your punches and really drive that power home.

## Boxing Footwork Tip #4

Lower your hands when out of range (yep, you read that correctly!)

The lower your center of gravity the quicker you'll be able to move around the ring. Now, in an actual bout I do not recommend dropping your hands down if your opponent is in your face attempting to walk you down – but as you avoid strikes and move laterally around the ring you'll conserve energy and increase your footwork speed and balance by lowering them. No need to drop them down by your sides, lowering from head height to chest height will suffice.

## Boxing Footwork Tip #5

Understand circling.

Using your lateral movement to circle your opponent instead of remaining a stationary target is a wise move, but you must understand which way you are circling…

Under no circumstance should you circle towards your opponent's rear hand.
Circling towards their rear hand is circling into their power – allowing them to time a straight right hand (or left in the instance of facing a southpaw).

You must circle away from their power hand – I've sparred many opponents that've circled towards my power hand and I've landed devastating blows as a result (coming out southpaw then quickly switching stance and throwing power shots while your adversary is circling away from the southpaw power hand is a sneaky tactic I like to employ from time to time).

If your adversary tries to throw their rear hand while you're circling away from it they'll likely misjudge the distance and end up missing and leaving themselves wide open for a counter or missing and potentially ending up off-balance… both situations you can use to your advantage.

## Boxing Footwork Tip #6

The size of the step you take with one foot is the same size you should take with the other.

This is a common mistake I see many beginner, intermediate and advanced boxers make to this day. They don't understand that in order to maintain a correct boxing stance if you step forward 5 inches with your left foot you should be stepping forward 5 inches with your rear foot and vice versa. Taking odd step sizes will result in your boxing stance being either too wide or too narrow – resulting in you missing out on an opportunity to counter your opponent or perhaps leaving you too narrow and off balance, resulting in you either being knocked down or potentially even just falling down. Not a good look.

# Chapter 9 – General Boxing Head Movement Tips

## Understanding Specific Head Movement Techniques:

### Left Slip

Pivot on your rear leg to the left while dropping your head slightly to the left.

### Right Slip

Pivot on your front leg to the right while dropping your head slightly to the right.

### Pull

Transfer the majority of your weight to your rear leg while pulling your head backwards ever so slightly (a couple of inches). If you find yourself feeling off balance while performing the pull then feel free to do a small step backwards with your rear leg to remain in a firm planted position.

<u>Duck</u>

While maintaining your boxing stance bend your knees slightly and lower the level of your head to ensure you are out of the way of any strikes that're headed your way.

**Understanding Head Movement Patterns:**

<u>Circles</u>

Circular head movement is just as it sounds, you're moving your head in a circle pattern – the thing most guys fail to understand is you do not need to use the full circle whenever you're moving your head – work within half the circle, a quarter of the circle, change it up to keep your opponent guessing to ensure they are never able to land a clean shot.

<u>Angles</u>

Angular head movement is as it sounds, using lines and angle patterns of head movement, working in small and large triangle shaped movements. I suggest becoming accustom to circular head movement before delving into the slightly more advanced angular style.

# Chapter 10 – Boxing Focus Mitt Drills

**Boxing Drill #1**
Jab
Jab
Cross

**Boxing Drill #2**
Jab
Cross
Left Hook

**Boxing Drill #3**
Jab
Jab
Shovel Hook

**Boxing Drill #4**
Jab
Jab
Cross
Left Uppercut
Left Hook

**Boxing Drill #5**
Jab
Right Uppercut
Cross
Left Hook

**Boxing Drill #6**
Left Uppercut
Right Uppercut
Left Uppercut
Right Uppercut
Shovel Hook
Left Hook

## Boxing Drill #7
Jab
Cross
Pad Holder throws jab & cross back while you slip to the left
followed by the right.
Jab
Cross

## Boxing Drill #8
Jab
Right Uppercut
Left Hook
Cross
Pad Holder throws jab & cross back while you slip to the left
followed by the right.
Shovel Hook

## Boxing Drill #9
Cross
Left Hook
Cross
Left Hook
Cross
Pad Holder throws left hook, weave under this.
Left Hook
Cross

## Boxing Drill #10
Jab
Jab
Shovel Hook
Pad Holder throws left hook, weave under this.
Cross
Left Hook
Right Uppercut

## Boxing Drill #11
Right Uppercut
Shovel Hook
Left Hook

Pad Holder throws jab & cross back while you slip to the left followed by the right.
Jab
Cross

**Boxing Drill #12**
Jab
Right Uppercut
Right Uppercut
Shovel Hook
Jab
Cross
Left Hook

**Boxing Drill #13**
Left Hook
Right Hook
Left Uppercut
Pad Holder throws left hook, weave under this.
Cross

**Boxing Drill #14**
Fast Jab
Fast Cross
Fast Jab
Powerful Cross
Pad Holder throws jab & cross back while you slip to the left followed by the right.
Powerful Cross

**Boxing Drill #15**
Jab
Cross
Shovel Hook
Shovel Hook
Right Uppercut
Left Hook

**Boxing Drill #16**
Shovel Hook

Left Uppercut
Left Hook
Cross
Right Uppercut

**Boxing Drill #17**
Jab
Cross
Pad Holder throws jab & cross, cover up by holding your
gloves tight against your face to block his punches.
Jab
Cross
Cross

**Boxing Drill #18**
Jab
Jab
Right Uppercut
Left Uppercut
Pad Holder throws left hook, weave under this.
Left Hook
Cross

**Boxing Drill #19**
Jab
Cross
Left Hook
Cross
Pad Holder throws left hook, weave under this.
Cross
Left Hook
Pad Holder throws left hook, weave under this.
Cross

**Boxing Drill #20**
Jab
Cross
Pad Holder throws jab & cross, cover up by holding your
gloves tight against your face to block his punches.
Jab

Cross
Pad Holder throws left hook, weave under this.
Jab
Right Uppercut
Left Uppercut

# Conclusion

Thank you again for purchasing my boxing book!

I hope you've found this book to be valuable; I can still vividly remember the day I stepped foot in a boxing gym with a dusty old pair of Everlast gloves that I picked up from a yard sale down the road from my parents' house.

As I mentioned in the introduction of this book I can equip you with all the knowledge in the world on how to improve your boxing skills but it's up to you to put this newly acquired knowledge to work with the techniques, tactics and drills you've now become familiar with.

Lastly, if you enjoyed this book I'd be ever so grateful if you could share your thoughts in a review on Amazon.com. It'd be greatly appreciated.

Best of luck on your journey my friend, now go out there and start grinding.

Frank Sasso.